Computers and Schools

Jim Drake

Heinemann Library
Chicago, Illinois

© 1999 Reed Educational & Professional Publishing
Published by Heinemann Library,
an imprint of Reed Educational & Professional Publishing,
100 North LaSalle, Suite 1010
Chicago, IL 60602
Customer Service: 888-454-2279
Visit our website at www.heinemannnlibrary.com

Designed by Visual Image
Printed in Hong Kong, China

03 02 01 00
10 9 8 7 6 5 4 3 2

Library of Congress Cataloging-in-Publication Data

Drake, Jim, 1955-
    Computers and school / Jim Drake.
      p. cm. -- (Log on to computers)
    Includes bibliographical references and index.
    Summary: A basic introduction to the use of computers in schools, describing word processing, desktop publishing, networks, computer—assisted learning, graphics, computer-produced music, and computer simulations.
    ISBN 1-57572-785-4 (lib. bdg.)
    1. Computer-assisted instruction—Juvenile literature.
2. Education (Primary)—Data processing—Juvenile literature.
3. Computers—Juvenile literature. [1. Computers.] I. Title.
II. Series: Drake, Jim, 1955- Log on to computers.
LB1028.5.D69   1999
372.133'4—dc21   98-48090
                                    CIP
                                      AC

Acknowledgments
The publishers would like to thank the following for permission to reproduce photographs:
John Birdsall Photography, p. 16; Bromcom Computers, p. 8; Trevor Clifford, pp. 6, 7, 9, 10, 11, 12, 13, 14, 18, 21 (both), 23, 24, 25; Format/Sally Lancaster, p. 17; Image Bank/V. Lange, p. 4; Katz Pictures/G. Smith, p. 27; NORTEL, p. 28; Science Photo Library/D. Lovegrove, p.19; D. Parker, p. 22; F. Sauze, p, 26; G Tompkinson, p. 29; John Walmsley, p. 5; Yamaha, p. 15.

Cover illustration by Andy Parker.

Every effort has been made to contact copyright holders of any material reproduced in this book. Any omissions will be rectified in subsequent printings if notice is given to the publisher.

Some words in this book are shown in bold, **like this.** You can find out what they mean by looking in the

CONTENTS

COMPUTERS NOW AND THEN

In 1980 there were few computers in schools. Today every school has them because it is important to learn about computers. People working in most jobs use computers now. Computers can help us learn about many things, too.

Your parents hardly used computers when they went to school.

Different **programs**, called **software**, can make one computer do many jobs. Computers can find information very quickly. They can even get it from the other side of the world. You can use computers for entertainment, too. You can play games, make pictures, and play music, all on the same computer.

Now, nearly all classrooms have computers.

WORD PROCESSORS

The computer has checked this letter. All the mistakes are highlighted.

This book was written on a computer using a **word processor**. A word processor is a writing **program**. When you type the words on a keyboard, they appear on the screen. Most word processors only work with **text.** Text means words, or writing.

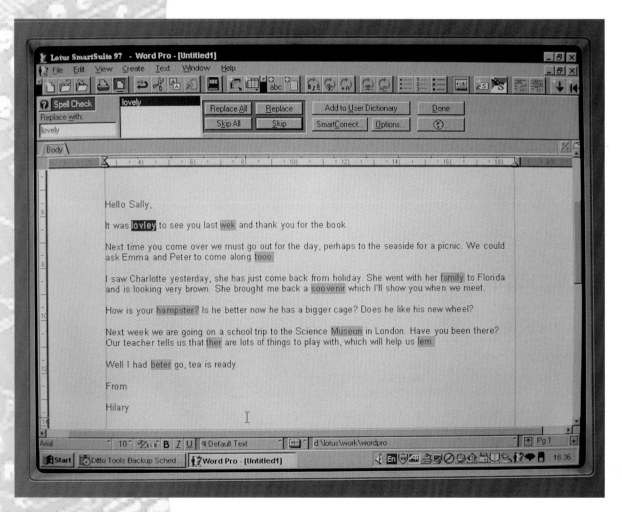

Hello Sally,

It was lovely to see you last week and thank you for the book.

Next time you come over we must go out for the day, perhaps to the seaside for a picnic. We could ask Emma and Peter to come along too.

I saw Charlotte yesterday, she has just come back from holiday. She went with her family to Florida and is looking very brown. She brought me back a souvenir which I'll show you when we meet.

How is your hamster? Is he better now he has a bigger cage? Does he like his new wheel?

Next week we are going on a school trip to the Science Museum in London. Have you been there? Our teacher tells us that there are lots of things to play with, which will help us learn.

Well I had better go, tea is ready.

From

Hilary

27 Station Road
Borehamwood
Herts

When everything is correct on the screen, you can print out your work on paper.

You can change how the words look, their size, and how they are arranged. You can save your work in the computer and finish it later. Most word processors can check to see if you have made spelling mistakes. They can even correct the mistakes for you.

COMPUTERS IN THE OFFICE

Attendance taken with a computer makes it easy to find out where everyone is.

Your school office probably has computers. They are used for keeping information to help run the school. Information about students, grades, and supplies is kept on these computers. Computers can also answer phones and send **e-mail** letters.

At school, your address is probably stored on a **database**. This is a way of keeping information. If the school needs to send your family a letter, the information is on the database. Letters from school are usually typed on a **word processor**.

Computers in the school office save time. It is quick and easy to type and print letters using a computer.

COMPUTER GRAPHICS

Graphics are pictures. Some **programs** can draw and change pictures. Computer programs can draw shapes in many colors. You can make as many changes as you want on the computer screen. When the picture looks right, you can print it out on paper.

These children have used a drawing program to help make this picture.

A **scanner** sends photographs or pictures to the computer. A drawing program on the computer can change the scanned picture. You can mix two pictures together. You can also make special effects, like stretching or twisting a picture.

The picture on the screen has been scanned from a photo. These children will soon change the way the picture looks.

DESKTOP PUBLISHING

Using a DTP program, you can move things on the screen until they are in the right spot.

DTP stands for "desktop publishing." DTP **programs** are like **word processors**, but they let you use pictures, too. You can make a page with **text** and **graphics.** It's like sticking pictures together to make a collage.

When you like what is on the screen, you can print it. Large projects can be sent on a **disk** to a printing company. Newspapers and books are usually made this way. Many schools make their own newspapers, magazines, or yearbooks using DTP.

You can change your work on screen, but you can't change it once it has been printed!

COMPUTERS AND MUSIC

Making music with a computer can be fun. Most computers have a **sound card** and loudspeakers. You can put music CDs in the computer and have music while you work! With the right **programs,** you can write songs and make the computer play them.

Today, most personal computers can play music.

Computers can be linked to electronic instruments, like keyboards or drum machines. Special **software** sends messages that make the instruments play the note you want. You can play or write songs and the computer will remember them. It can play them back for you.

With special software, a computer can play two or more instruments at the same time.

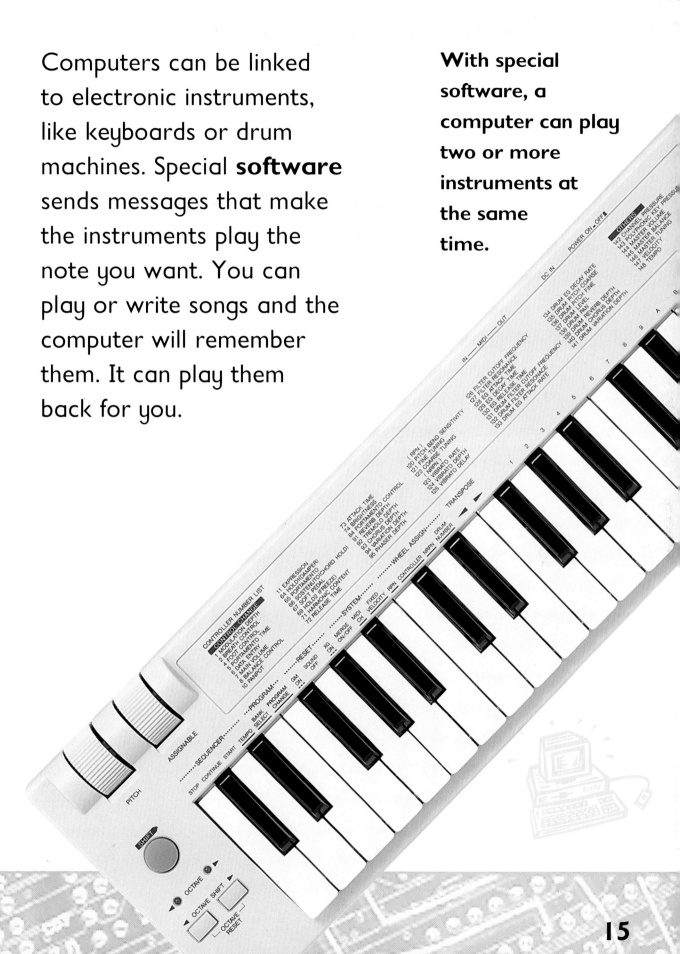

COMPUTERS AND DISABILITY

Computers help students with **disabilities**. If a person cannot hold a pencil or pen easily, a computer can help them to write. They don't even need to be able to type. Computers can also turn spoken words into writing. Some "speak" words written down on paper.

Some computers don't need keyboards. This one is controlled by breathing.

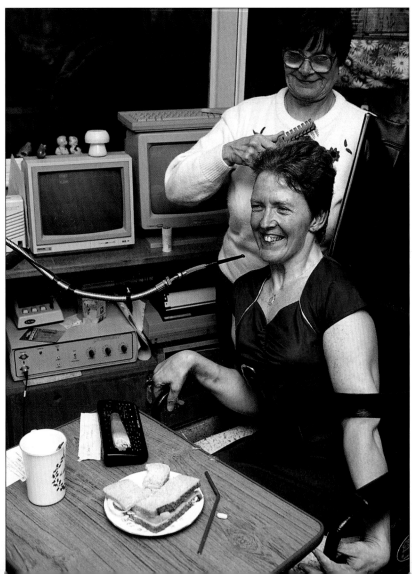

Computers help people in school to move around. Some people can't move enough to steer an electric wheelchair. They can steer their wheelchairs by blowing and sucking down a special tube. **Software** in the computer recognizes the pattern of sucks and blows and moves the motors on the wheelchair.

This computer helps a blind student to read. Its software sees the printed words and "speaks" them into the headphones that the man is wearing.

CD-ROMS

Some **CD-ROMs have** encyclopedias. **Students can find** information on many subjects on one **CD-ROM.**

A **CD-ROM** looks like a music CD. It is like a book that you can read with a computer. One CD-ROM can contain the words and pictures from many books. This can make it quick and easy to look up things. CD-ROMs can also have sounds and moving pictures on them.

CD-ROMs cannot be used at all without a computer. A book works anywhere! You can now get rewritable CD-ROMs that can save your own work or move it to another computer. CD-ROMs are also used to put **software** on to a computer.

Unlike books, **CD-ROMs can** contain videos and music, as well as words and pictures.

NETWORKS

If your school has many computers, it may have a **network**. A network joins many computers together. There is usually one big computer called a server. The server stores most of the **programs** and the work that people do. The computers where people do their work are called workstations.

The server sends information and programs to the workstations when they are needed. All of the computers on a network can use one printer. Messages can be sent from one computer to another through the server. You can even play computer games with someone else on the network.

In this school,
the computers
are all joined
in a network.
The biggest
computer is the
server. It sends
messages to
the rest of the
network.

THE INTERNET

Is your school connected to the **Internet?** If it is, you will be able to find out things from all over the world. The Internet is like a **network** covering the whole world. You can send **e-mail** to people anywhere in the world and find out how they live.

This man is putting information on the World Wide Web. It can be read by people all over the world.

With a special camera and microphone linked to a computer, you can even see and hear other people. On the **World Wide Web** you can get information from millions of other computers. There is so much information that it is sometimes hard to find what you want.

This is a web page from the Internet. The underlined words can connect you to other pages and sites on the Internet.

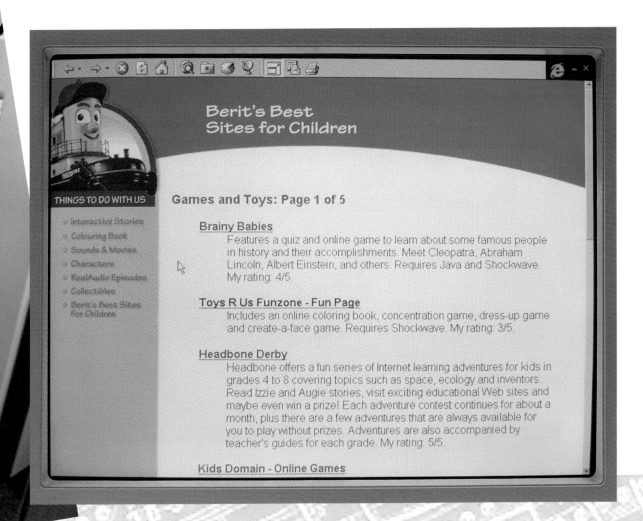

Berit's Best
Sites for Children

THINGS TO DO WITH US
- Interactive Stories
- Colouring Book
- Sounds & Movies
- Characters
- RealAudio Episodes
- Collectibles
- Berit's Best Sites For Children

Games and Toys: Page 1 of 5

Brainy Babies
  Features a quiz and online game to learn about some famous people in history and their accomplishments. Meet Cleopatra, Abraham Lincoln, Albert Einstein, and others. Requires Java and Shockwave. My rating: 4/5.

Toys R Us Funzone - Fun Page
  Includes an online coloring book, concentration game, dress-up game and create-a-face game. Requires Shockwave. My rating: 3/5.

Headbone Derby
  Headbone offers a fun series of Internet learning adventures for kids in grades 4 to 8 covering topics such as space, ecology and inventors. Read Izzie and Augie stories, visit exciting educational Web sites and maybe even win a prize! Each adventure contest continues for about a month, plus there are a few adventures that are always available for you to play without prizes. Adventures are also accompanied by teacher's guides for each grade. My rating: 5/5.

Kids Domain - Online Games

COMPUTER-ASSISTED LEARNING

In this classroom, some children are learning with the teacher, while the others are using a computer to learn.

Some computer **programs** help you learn without a teacher. This is called Computer-Assisted Learning, or CAL. The computer shows you how to do something. It can ask questions to make sure that you have understood.

If you get the answers right, you can go on to the next question. Sometimes, to make it fun, the questions are part of a game. The computer can help you to learn at the right speed for you. Computers help real teachers do their jobs.

Computers can help make learning fun.

COMPUTER SIMULATIONS

Simulations can be fun. Play simulations are usually easier than the real thing.

Sometimes people need to learn special skills. Computer simulations can help teach how to drive cars and fly aircraft. In a car simulation, you use controls, like a steering wheel, and the computer screen shows the scene you would see if you were really driving.

Astronauts use simulators to practice. Real rocket launches are too dangerous and expensive to do as practice.

A lot of computer games are like this, but simulations are more realistic. Simulations help people to learn skills that would be too dangerous or expensive to practice in other ways. If you crash in a simulation, no one gets hurt and you don't do any damage.

NO MORE SCHOOL?

One day, all schoolwork might be done at home.

Computers are getting faster and more powerful all the time. Some people think that one day, there will be no schools. Everyone will learn at home using computers.

You may use the **Internet** and **CD-ROMs** instead of books. Students might talk to teachers on computer screens. But it might be boring and lonely if there was no one else around. What do you think?

Some games already use **virtual reality.** Students may use it to explore places that they could never go to in real life.

GLOSSARY

CD-ROM   shiny disc that can store words, pictures, and music

database   software that holds information that can be collected quickly and in many ways

disability not being able to do something in a normal way

disk   small movable device that holds computer programs and information

e-mail   electronic mail messages sent between computers

Internet network of computers around the world through which information is shared

network   group of computers that are connected and able to share information and equipment

program instructions that tell a computer what to do

scanner machine that turns pictures on paper into computer code

software another name for the programs that tell a computer what to do

sound card computer part that allows it to play music and make other sounds

Text another name for words or writing

virtual reality computer-created "world" in which sights and sounds seem real and the user can interact

word processor software that helps people to write

World Wide Web way of getting information from other computers through the Internet

Index

More Books to Read

Kalman, Bobbie. *The Computer from A to Z.* New York: N.Y.: Crabtree Publishing Company, 1998.

Kazunas, Charnan and Thomas Kazunas. *The Internet for Kids.* Danbury, Conn.: Children's Press, 1997.

Steinhauser, Peggy L. *Mousetracks: A Kid's Computer Idea Book.* Berkeley, Cal.: Tricycle Press, 1997.